Kids Read and Write Japanese Haiku

by VA Rivera

Introduce kids ages 8 and older to poetry with simple Japanese Haiku.

Discover themes and syllable patterns. Kids are encouraged to

use model poems to write their own. Great for parents, teachers, or

anyone helping kids learn an appreciation for the art of poetry.

Publishing Services by:
Telemachus Press, LLC
7652 Sawmill Road, Suite 304
Dublin, Ohio 43016

ISBN: 978-1-965121-24-5
Version: 20250526

Introduction: What is a Japanese Haiku?

Welcome to the wonderful world of Japanese Haiku! Japanese Haiku poems are short poems that were first written in Japan hundreds of years ago.

Readers usually notice Haiku do not rhyme. Haiku also have a total of three lines.

The first and second lines of a Japanese Haiku usually use images and words to describe the subject. The third line of a Haiku is for a metaphor, simile, or personification. When writing Japanese Haiku in English ...

The first line has five syllables. (Descriptive Words/Images)

The second line has seven syllables. (Descriptive Words/Images)

The third line has five syllables. (Metaphor, Simile, or Personification)

Japanese Haiku are usually about nature. In this book, the author chooses not to use this usual rule of Haiku and writes about other subjects. And that, my friends, is part of what makes writing poetry so much fun! Poets can use their creativity and imagination! Poets can follow poetry rules or not!

Read Kids Read and Write Japanese Haiku to help you learn how Haiku are written. I hope you will feel inspired to write your own! Play with words. Use your senses. Use your emotions. Use your wonderful imagination to create a new Japanese Haiku.

Just remember to have fun!

Chapter 1 Fun Haiku Poems

Kids **and** adults enjoy having fun. Fun activities cause kids to smile and feel happy. What are some fun activities kids enjoy with other kids?

Do you think it's possible to have fun, smile and feel happy by yourself? Tell someone near you one activity that you enjoy doing alone.

Read the following Fun Haiku Poems.

Running

Give me open space

to run and run and not look

back where I started

Hopscotch

Chalk-drawn boxes on

cement labeled with numbers

makes me skip and jump

Street Game

Kick the rubber ball

hard then run for your life 'round

bases touching home

Birthdays

Open presents eat

cake ice cream chips and dip play

Pin the Tail on the Donkey

In Chapter 1 you learned about Fun Japanese Haiku Poems. Now it's your turn to write one of your own! First choose the fun to write about. Remember to use the 5/7/5 pattern of syllables! Share your Haiku with a friend, an adult you know, or a teacher.

Chapter 2 Nature Haiku Poems

Bird Haiku Poems are filled with feathers and wings and songs that sing many different tunes. Imagine walking through the woods and hearing the little birds whispering. Are they sharing jokes or perhaps recipes? Are they chatting about the weather?

Maybe talking birds teach about doing good to neighbors, or simply just listen to you when you are sad. The forest, the trees, the branches, the leaves and every animal or insect living there are always perfect subjects for Haiku Poems.

Singing Bird Haiku

In the day's morning

the sun shines golden and bright

as bird song warms us

Bird Melodies Haiku

Bird melodies bring

joy to my ears with peace I

wish the world to hear

Think about what you know about birds or trees or branches or leaves or any part of the forest. What would your Haiku Poem sound like?

Here are two examples:

Dancing Leaves

Leaves flutter and float

like twirling ballerinas

drifting in the air

Autumn Leaves

I ask the rainbow

who paints the Autumn colors

but she will not tell

In Chapter 2 you learned about Nature Japanese Haiku Poems. I am certain you can write one of your own! First choose something from nature to write about. Remember to use the 5/7/5 pattern of syllables! Share your Haiku with a friend, an adult you know, or a teacher.

Chapter 3 Space Haiku Poems

Silence in Space

Quiet can be loud

when something interrupts it

like listening ears

Lost in Space

In the home of the

stars silence is everywhere

like a moon-lit night

In Chapter 3 you read Japanese Haiku Poems about Space. Now it's your turn to write one of your own! First choose something in or about Space for your poem's main idea. Remember to use the 5/7/5 pattern of syllables! Share your Haiku with a friend, an adult you know, or a teacher!

Chapter 4 Imagination Haiku Poems

Now you will go on a journey of your creative mind where fantastical creatures live. You will read haiku Poems about Unicorns, or rainbows, or mermaids. What kind of creature can you create?

Unicorns

Unicorns dance on

the green grass by the silvery

pond with so much joy

Rainbows

When rain stops and you

say goodbye to the storm clouds

blue skies smi-le wide

Mermaids

Soup is salty when

mermaids add sea water for

much needed flavor

In Chapter 4 you learned to use your imagination in Japanese Haiku Poems. Now it's your turn to write one of your own! First choose a subject under the sea to write about. Remember to use the 5/7/5 pattern of syllables! Share your Haiku with a friend, an adult you know, or a teacher!

Chapter 5 Under the Sea

Welcome to ... under the sea. Imagine the glorious and colorful creatures you might find in a deep dive into the wonders of the ocean. Put on your underwater mask along with the rest of your scuba gear. Get ready to imagine swimming with living creatures. What might you see beneath the waves?

Listen, read and wonder with these three Japanese Haiku poems: Regal Seahorse, Funny Octopus, and Graceful Sea Turtle. Each creature has a story, and each poem paints a beautiful picture.

Regal Seahorse

Queen of the ocean

eating shrimp all the day long

but has no stomach

Brine shrimp her servants

give their lives as food for a

much beloved Queen

Funny Octopus

Octi has arms for

giving love hugs and squeezes

on Valentine's Day

One Octopus or

many will squirt ink to be

safely protected

Graceful Sea Turtles

We are cold-blooded

beach loving rep-ti-les that

love a good suntan

Racoons, foxes, and

birds steal mama's eggs laid on

the sandy shoreline

In Chapter 5 you read Japanese Haiku Poems about the sea. Now imagine in your mind a picture of a sea creature you would like to write about in your own Japanese Haiku. What is the creature doing? If no creature comes to mind, create a new one of your own!

Remember to use the 5/7/5 pattern of syllables! Share your Haiku with a friend, an adult you know, or a teacher!

Chapter 6 Friend Haiku Poems

Friendship means sticking by your side through thick and thin. You have someone who laughs with you, cries with you, and shares each other's secrets.

A friend always has your back. A friend will support you, defend you, stick up for you. You can always count on a friend!

Together you and your friend keep each other safe. You and your friend are always comfortable with each other. If someone or something makes either of you uncomfortable, you need an adult you trust to help you. When you are afraid, together you can always find your brave.

A friend will try new things with you or share quiet moments. Together you celebrate. Together you sing. Together you learn. Everything is better with a friend on whom you can rely.

I Cherish My Friend Haiku

We laugh together

cry together my friend is

my steady anchor

We help each other

be the best person we can

be through thick or thin

A Friend is a Gift Haiku

A friend is a gift

a priceless treasure for me

to keep close always

More valuable than

red rubies or bright diamonds

like a precious gem

You may have a friend in mind right now. Even if you don't, imagine how you would want a new friend to be. How do you want to feel about a friend? Now try writing your own Friend Haiku, maybe about a friend you have or a friend you hope to have one day!

Something to do:

Make a new friend by sharing your Friend Haiku with someone new!

In Chapter 6 you read Japanese Haiku Poems about Friendship and even tried your hand at writing one!

Now imagine yourself as a little child. It's the end of a long day. You are tired and ready for bedtime.

Chapter 7 Bedtime Lullaby Haiku Poems

Many babies and little children love to hear sweet goodnight melodies called lullabies. Lullabies calm babies and little children to help them fall asleep.

Do you remember any lullabies someone might have sung to you? What might a good lullaby for a baby or little child sound like? Think about words you might use or messages to say that will help relax and calm a baby or little child. Do you think a melody can be a lullaby without words?

Read the following examples of Lullaby Haiku Poems:

Good Night

Good night to all the

little ones sleeping on clouds

like pillows on high

Good night the rain is

gone from clouds turning them to

whitest fluffy puffs

Dreams

May dreams of gentle

angel songs and harps fill your

mind with calm and ease

May dreams be sweetest

ever had among the stars

shining in night's sky

Think about a Lullaby Haiku Poem you would like to write. Remember the poem is for a baby or little child who needs to rest. What might be some calming words or messages that would help sleep to come.

Try writing your own Lullaby Haiku Poem. Remember to use the 5/7/5 pattern of syllables!

Share your Haiku with a friend, an adult you know, or a teacher - be careful not to fall asleep!

You have come to the end of your introduction to <u>Kids Read and Write Japanese Haiku</u> ... but this is not the end of creating new Haiku Poems!

You know how to recognize and write Japanese Haiku Poems so you can write a Japanese Haiku Poem on just about any subject!

Congratulations on becoming a poet of Japanese Haiku Poems!

Never stop learning and keep on writing!

About the Author

VA Rivera is a retired educator who loves poetry and laughing out loud. VA Rivera lives happily in Yonkers, New York with a gentle pastel calico named HoneyBun and a feisty Tiger Stripe named SweetiePie.

VA spent 30 years teaching children how to read and write different types of poems. Many class collections were published, and every child created a poetry journal to bring home and keep forever.

VA continues to write her own poetry that she workshops with a favorite online group of the most wonderful poets. VA encourages all children to read and write their own original poetry.

Share with me the Japanese Haiku poems you write! I would love to read your favorites!

Email me: va_rivera@varivera.com

Website: www.varivera.com

"If you read poems you will learn to understand poems. If you learn to understand poems, you will learn to love poetry." VA Rivera